TEAM SPIRIT ®

SMART BOOKS FOR YOUNG FANS

THE NEW YORK RANGERS

BY

MARK STEWART

CONTENT CONSULTANT
DENIS GIBBONS
SOCIETY FOR INTERNATIONAL HOCKEY RESEARCH

NORWOOD HOUSE PRESS

CHICAGO, ILLINOIS

Norwood House Press
P.O. Box 316598
Chicago, Illinois 60631

For information regarding Norwood House Press, please visit our website at:
www.norwoodhousepress.com or call 866-565-2900.

All photos courtesy of Associated Press except the following:
McDiarmid/Cartophilium (7), Hockey Hall of Fame (8), Black Book Partners (9, 23, 43 bottom right),
Getty Images (10, 11, 12, 32, 41), Topps, Inc. (15, 17, 21, 30, 34 left, 35 top left, 38, 40, 42 top),
Author's Collection (22, 33, 34 right, 43 bottom left), Bee Hive Golden Corn Syrup/Cargill, Inc. (28),
The Upper Deck Company (35 top right), TIME Inc./Sports Illustrated for Kids (35 bottom),
The Quarton Group/NHL (36), Acme Photos (37), Beckett Publications (39, 42 bottom),
O-Pee-Chee Ltd. (43 top, 45).
Cover Photo: AP Photo/Frank Franklin II

The memorabilia and artifacts pictured in this book are presented for educational and informational purposes,
and come from the collection of the author.

Editor: Mike Kennedy
Designer: Ron Jaffe
Project Management: Black Book Partners, LLC.
Special thanks to Topps, Inc.

Library of Congress Cataloging-in-Publication Data

Stewart, Mark, 1960 July 7-
    The New York Rangers / by Mark Stewart. -- Revised edition.
       pages cm. -- (Team spirit)
    Includes bibliographical references and index.
    Summary: "A revised Team Spirit Hockey edition featuring the New York
    Rangers that chronicles the history and accomplishments of the team.
    Includes access to the Team Spirit website which provides additional
    information and photos"-- Provided by publisher.
      ISBN 978-1-59953-624-8 (library edition : alk. paper) -- ISBN
    978-1-60357-632-1 (ebook) 1. New York Rangers (Hockey
    team)--History--Juvenile literature 2. Hockey teams--United
    States--History--Juvenile literature. I. Title.
      GV848.N43S74 2014
      796.962'647471--dc23

                                            2013034898

© 2014 by Norwood House Press.
Team Spirit® is a registered trademark of Norwood House Press.
All rights reserved.
No part of this book may be reproduced without written permission from the publisher.
•
The New York Rangers is a registered trademark of MSG Holdings, L.P.
This publication is not affiliated with MSG Holdings, L.P.,
The National Hockey League, or The National Hockey League Players Association.

Manufactured in the United States of America in Stevens Point, Wisconsin.
239N—012014

COVER PHOTO: The Rangers rush onto the ice to celebrate a victory during
the 2012–13 season.

TABLE OF CONTENTS

ABOUT OUR GLOSSARY

In this book, there may be several words that you are reading for the first time. Some are sports words, some are new vocabulary words, and some are familiar words that are used in an unusual way. All of these words are defined on page 46. Throughout the book, sports words appear in **bold type**. Regular vocabulary words appear in ***bold italic type***.

MEET THE RANGERS

Competition in the **National Hockey League (NHL)** is fast and furious. Competition among the sports teams in New York can be just as fierce. The New York Rangers are one of nine major sports teams in the area. They all compete for fans.

To be successful, the Rangers need to find the right mix of superstars and supporting players. The top players often grab the headlines, while their less-famous teammates do the hard work that a hockey team needs to win close games. When all the pieces fall into place, the result is almost magical.

This book tells the story of the Rangers. They have had some of the greatest stars in hockey history, plus some of the most loyal fans in all of sports. Through more than 80 years of ups and downs, the Rangers have held a special place in the hearts of New Yorkers and in the history of New York.

Ryan Callahan jumps for joy—and gets a squeeze from Anton Stralman— after scoring a game-winning goal against the Carolina Hurricanes.

GLORY DAYS

During the early 1900s, hockey became very popular in New York City. Fans rushed to buy tickets to watch the best **professional** and **amateur** talent on the ice. In 1925, a sports promoter named Tex Rickard built a new arena on the West Side of Manhattan in New York City and called it Madison Square Garden. Rickard filled the seats by staging basketball games, cycling races, boxing matches, and the ever-popular circus. An NHL team called the Americans played its games in the Garden and drew enormous crowds. Rickard soon decided to start his own team.

The NHL was anxious to spread south from Canada and move into major American cities. Placing another team in New York was a welcome idea. Rickard's club was nicknamed "Tex's Rangers" (which sounded like a famous group of western lawmen from Texas). The Rangers joined the NHL for the 1926–27 season. Two of hockey's greatest pioneers, Conn Smythe and Lester Patrick, assembled the **roster** and ran the club.

The Rangers were a hit from the very beginning. Many entertainment celebrities attended their games, and Rickard saw to it that his players were paid well and treated well. In 1929, the Rangers became the first hockey team to travel to their games by airplane.

New York's early stars included Frank Boucher and the Cook brothers, Bill and Fred, whose nickname was "Bun." Together they formed the high-scoring "Bread **Line**." The defense was anchored by Ching Johnson. When Patrick took over as coach in the team's second season, the Rangers won their first **Stanley Cup**. They repeated as champions in 1933. By the end of the 1930s, Patrick's two sons—Lynn and Muzz—were stars for the Rangers. So were two other brothers, Neil and Mac Colville. Along with Phil Watson, Bryan Hextall, Clint Smith, and goalie Davey Kerr, they made the

LEFT: Tex Rickard steadies the heavy bag for boxing champ Jack Dempsey.
ABOVE: This trading card shows Neil Colville, one of the team's stars during the 1940s.

Rangers almost unbeatable. New York won the Stanley Cup in 1940, with Boucher coaching the team.

In the years after World War II, the Rangers had some great players, but they tumbled in the **standings**. The team's stars during this *era* included Andy Bathgate and Dean Prentice. Goalie Gump Worsley and Harry Howell led the defense. By the late 1960s, the Rangers ranked among the top teams in the league again. Goalie Ed Giacomin and defenseman Brad Park protected the New York net. Jean Ratelle, Rod Gilbert, and Vic Hadfield formed the "GAG Line"—which stood for goal-a-game. Other stars included forwards Walt Tkaczuk, Bobby Rousseau, and Billy Fairbairn, and goalie Gilles Villameure. In 1972, the Rangers reached the **Stanley Cup Finals** for the first time since 1950.

At the end of the 1970s, a remade lineup took the team back to the finals. New York's stars included Phil Esposito, Don Maloney,

LEFT: Ed Giacomin was one of the most popular Rangers ever.
ABOVE: Brad Park holds the puck behind the net, as Rod Gilbert and Jean Ratelle get ready to head up the ice.

Ron Greschner, Carol Vadnais, Ron Duguay, John Davidson, and two fast-skating Swedes, Ulf Nilsson and Anders Hedberg. New York blended European and North American styles to create a whole new kind of hockey. Unfortunately, the 1980s belonged to the team's bitter rival, the New York Islanders, and later the Edmonton Oilers.

At the start of the 1990s, a half-century had passed since the Rangers last claimed the NHL championship. The club decided the best way to change its luck was to rebuild around a core of talented young players. Their leader was defenseman Brian Leetch, who was sensational at both ends of the ice. Leetch was joined on defense by a creative playmaker named Sergei Zubov. Playing the Rangers was often like having five forwards attacking the net.

The rest of the team was just as good. Mike Richter was a fearless young goalie. On the front line, Adam Graves was a hard-hitting forward with a good scoring touch. The team captain was Mark Messier, who was already a legendary leader. Prior to the 1993–94 season, the Rangers hired coach Mike Keenan to put these pieces together and complete the picture. By the end of the year, the Rangers were Stanley Cup champions.

Wayne Gretzky joined the team two years later, and it looked as if the Rangers were ready to build a *dynasty*. But age and injuries kept them from reaching their *potential*. The Rangers continued to add big stars, including Pat LaFontaine, Theo Fleury, Eric Lindros, and Pavel Bure. But instead of ruling the NHL, the Rangers failed to reach the **playoffs** seven years in a row starting in 1997–98. It was time for a new *generation* to take over.

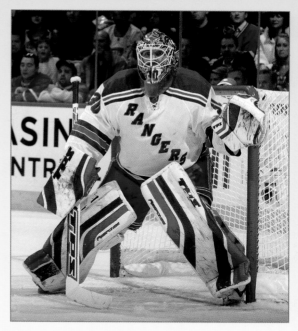

Starting in 2005–06, the Rangers posted eight winning seasons in a row. Their star player was Henrik Lundqvist, a goalie who made jaw-dropping saves night after night. The Rangers surrounded him with hungry young players, including Ryan Callahan, Derek Stepan, Brandon Dubinsky, Brian Boyle, Carl Hagelin, and Dan Girardi. They also brought in experienced stars, such as Rick Nash, Brad Richards, and Marian Gaborik. In 2011–12, New York won its **di..i..n** for the first time since its Stanley Cup season and made it all the way to the **conference** finals. The Rangers and their fans set their sights on the Stanley Cup once again.

LEFT: Many fans believe that Brian Leetch was the best defenseman in team history.   **ABOVE**: Henrik Lundqvist led the way for a new era of success in New York.

HOME ICE

The Rangers have had two homes during their long history. Both were named Madison Square Garden, even though neither arena was actually located on New York's Madison Square. The Rangers are nicknamed the Broadway Blues, although Broadway—the city's most famous street—was a block away from each building.

The new Madison Square Garden opened in 1968. Four *decades* later, that "new" building was the oldest arena in New York. Some said the Garden should be torn down and rebuilt so that the train station underneath could be enlarged. Others just wanted to modernize it. A compromise was made and the arena was updated, but the city also informed the team owners that they would have to find a new home for the Garden in 10 years.

BY THE NUMBERS

- *There are 17,200 seats for hockey in the Rangers' arena.*
- *The arena is the fourth building called Madison Square Garden. The first was built in 1879—and was actually located on Madison Square.*
- *The first sports event held in the current Rangers' arena was a basketball game between the Knicks and the San Diego Rockets.*

The Rangers honor Adam Graves at Madison Square Garden in 2009 by retiring his number.

DRESSED FOR SUCCESS

The Rangers' sweater has changed little over the 80-plus years since the team first took the ice. New York's colors have always been red, white, and blue. When the Rangers wear their blue sweater, the team name is spelled out diagonally in red letters. When the players wear white, the lettering is blue.

The Rangers were the first team to match their gloves to their uniforms. They have worn red, white, and blue gloves since 1957–58. The team has experimented with different designs and *logos* from time to time. In the late 1970s, the Rangers had a shield on the front of their sweaters. In the 1990s, the sweater showed the head of the Statue of Liberty.

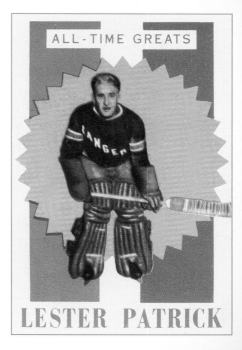

ALL-TIME GREATS

LESTER PATRICK

LEFT: Dan Girardi wears the team's away uniform during the 2012–13 season.   **RIGHT**: This trading card shows Lester Patrick in "Broadway Blue" from New York's early years.

WE WON!

When the Rangers joined the NHL, there were a lot of good hockey players in North America, but not a lot of teams paying high salaries. The bright lights and big paychecks of New York helped the Rangers build a good team very quickly. The club did especially well signing stars from the struggling **Western Canada Hockey League (WCHL)**. Frank Boucher, Bill Cook, and Bun Cook came from the WCHL. So did New York's coach, Lester Patrick. Goalie Lorne Chabot joined the Rangers after playing for a small-town team in Canada.

In 1927–28, Boucher and the Cooks formed the league's top line. They combined for 55 goals in 44 games. In the **postseason**, the Rangers beat the Pittsburgh Pirates and Boston Bruins to reach the Stanley Cup Finals against the Montreal Maroons. Because the circus was performing in Madison Square Garden, the series had to be played in Montreal.

The Rangers dropped Game 1. Then Chabot suffered an eye injury in Game 2. New York was in deep trouble. Teams did not carry extra goalies in those days. The white-haired Patrick had no choice but to

Frank Boucher was the star of the 1928 playoffs, with seven goals.

ALL-TIME GREATS

FRANK BOUCHER

tend goal himself. Patrick was amazing, stopping all but one of the 19 shots the Maroons fired at him. Boucher scored in **overtime** for a dramatic victory. The Rangers rolled from there. Joe Miller took over for Patrick in goal, and New York won its first Stanley Cup.

By 1933, New York's stars were all aging. But as the playoffs began, Boucher and the Cook brothers got their second wind. They beat the Montreal Canadiens and Detroit Red Wings to set up a championship showdown with the Toronto Maple Leafs. The Rangers won the Stanley Cup on an overtime goal by Bill Cook in Game 4. It was the first time in NHL history that the championship was decided in "OT."

New York captured its next title in 1940. Bryan Hextall was one of the NHL's fastest skaters. Neil Colville was a great scorer. Goalie Davey Kerr played his best when the Rangers had their backs against the wall. After a tough series win over the Boston Bruins, New York faced a championship rematch with Toronto.

The Rangers and Maple Leafs were evenly matched. Hextall scored a **hat trick** in Game 2 to give New York a win and the series lead. But Toronto tied it up with back-to-back victories. The Rangers won the next two games—and the Stanley Cup—on overtime goals by Muzz Patrick and Hextall.

No one could have imagined it then, but more than 50 years would pass before the Rangers hoisted the Stanley Cup again. In 1993–94, three superstars joined forces to make the Rangers champions. Mark Messier was a great leader who could lift his teammates when they were down. Brian Leetch was an excellent defenseman who loved to attack the net on offense. Goalie Mike Richter was one of the best in the game.

Under coach Mike Keenan, these stars blended with a strong supporting cast. The Rangers finished the season with the NHL's best record. They played with great confidence in playoff victories over the New York Islanders and Washington Capitals. In the Eastern Conference Finals, New York trailed the New Jersey Devils. But the Rangers rallied to win the series on Stephane Matteau's dramatic goal in Game 7.

The Rangers faced the Vancouver Canucks in the Stanley Cup Finals. New York fans worried when their team lost Game 1. However, the Rangers fought back and won three games in a row.

The Canucks tied the series to force Game 7 in New York. Leetch gave the Rangers a 1–0 lead with a goal in the first period, and Richter made several incredible saves in the third period. New York celebrated a 3–2 victory, and its fourth Stanley Cup. Leetch won the Conn Smythe Trophy as the **Most Valuable Player (MVP)** of the playoffs. Many elderly Rangers fans had feared they might not live long enough to see their team lift the Stanley Cup again. After the final siren sounded, one fan held a sign that read: NOW I CAN DIE IN PEACE.

LEFT: Mike Richter stretches to make a save against the Vancouver Canucks.
ABOVE: Mark Messier shows the Stanley Cup to the New York fans.

GO-TO GUYS

To be a true star in the NHL, you need more than a great slapshot. You have to be a "go-to guy"—someone teammates trust to make the winning play when the seconds are ticking away in a big game. Rangers fans have had a lot to cheer about over the years, including these great stars.

THE PIONEERS

FRANK BOUCHER   Center

- BORN: 10/7/1902 • DIED: 12/12/1977
- PLAYED FOR TEAM: 1926–27 TO 1937–38 & 1943–44

Frank Boucher was one of hockey's greatest playmakers. He was also one of the game's true gentlemen. Boucher won the Lady Byng Trophy for sportsmanship so often that the league let him keep the trophy, and then made a new one!

ANDY BATHGATE   Right Wing

- BORN: 8/28/1932 • PLAYED FOR TEAM: 1952–53 TO 1963–64

Andy Bathgate was a great leader. Even though the Rangers missed the playoffs in 1958–59, he still won the Hart Trophy as the league MVP. Bathgate had one of the NHL's hardest shots. He once set a record by scoring a goal in 10 games in a row.

HARRY HOWELL Defenseman

- BORN: 12/28/1932 • PLAYED FOR TEAM: 1952–53 TO 1968–69

Harry Howell played more games in a Rangers uniform than anyone in history. His nickname was "Harry the Horse" because he never seemed to get tired. Howell won the Norris Trophy as the NHL's best defenseman at the age of 35 and later was voted into the **Hall of Fame**.

ROD GILBERT Right Wing

- BORN: 7/1/1941 • PLAYED FOR TEAM: 1960–61 TO 1977–78

Rod Gilbert fought through the pain of a back injury to become a star. During his career, he needed two major operations to continue playing. He still managed to score more than 400 goals for the Rangers and retired with more than 1,000 points (goals plus **assists**).

ED GIACOMIN Goalie

- BORN: 6/6/1939 • PLAYED FOR TEAM: 1965–66 TO 1975–76

New York fans adored Ed Giacomin. The Rangers made the playoffs nine times during his 10 years as a starter. He led the NHL in wins three times. Giacomin was so reliable that fans nicknamed him "Steady Eddie."

BRAD PARK Defenseman

- BORN: 7/6/1948 • PLAYED FOR TEAM: 1968–69 TO 1975–76

Brad Park was one of the NHL's best "offensive" defensemen. He was also superb in his own end. Instead of slamming into forwards, Park muscled them to spots where they had to give up the puck.

ABOVE: Harry Howell

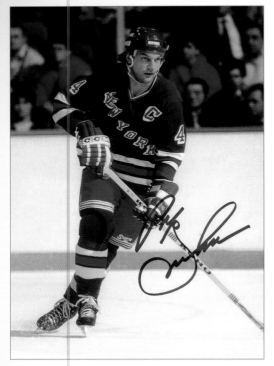

RON GRESCHNER — Defenseman

- BORN: 11/22/1954
- PLAYED FOR TEAM: 1974–75 TO 1989–90

After the Rangers traded Brad Park, Ron Greschner became the team's leader on defense. He scored three game-winning goals during the 1979 playoffs. Greschner was one of the most popular and glamorous athletes in New York when he played.

BRIAN LEETCH — Defenseman

- BORN: 3/3/1968
- PLAYED FOR TEAM: 1987–88 TO 2003–04

Brian Leetch was a top defenseman and an equally talented offensive player. He had a hard, accurate shot and was a skilled passer. Leetch won the Norris Trophy twice and set a record for first-year defensemen with 23 goals.

MIKE RICHTER — Goalie

- BORN: 9/22/1966   • PLAYED FOR TEAM: 1989–90 TO 2002–03

The more pressure opponents put on Mike Richter, the calmer he seemed to get. His great play in the 1994 playoffs was a key to the Rangers' long-awaited Stanley Cup. Richter and Brian Leetch were two of the top American stars in the NHL during the 1990s.

MARK MESSIER Center

- BORN 1/18/1961
- PLAYED FOR TEAM: 1991–92 TO 1996–97
  & 2000–01 TO 2003–04

Mark Messier was one of the greatest leaders in hockey history. He was a fierce and focused player who lifted the Rangers to the top of the NHL. Messier scored 107 points in his first season in New York and played in the **All-Star Game** three times.

HENRIK LUNDQVIST Goalie

- BORN: 3/2/ 1982 • FIRST SEASON WITH TEAM: 2005–06

Henrik Lundqvist continued New York's *tradition* of great goaltenders. He won at least 30 games in each of his first seven seasons to set an NHL record. In 2011–12, Lundqvist earned the Vezina Trophy as the league's best goalie.

RYAN CALLAHAN Right Wing

- BORN: 3/21/1985 • FIRST SEASON WITH TEAM: 2006–07

Ryan Callahan came up through the **minor leagues** with Dan Girardi. The pair gave New York two tough players who helped them return to the playoffs in 2007. Callahan scored four goals in a game in 2011 and led the Rangers to the Eastern Conference Finals in 2012.

LEFT: Ron Greschner signed this photo showing him wearing the captain's C.
ABOVE: Mark Messier watches the game from the bench.

The Rangers have had more than 30 coaches in their history. Among the best were Lester Patrick, Emile Francis, Fred Shero, Herb Brooks, Mike Keenan, and Roger Neilson. All rank among the finest coaches in NHL history. Many former star players have also coached the team, including Frank Boucher, Bill Cook, Neil Colville, Phil Watson, Phil Esposito, and Glen Sather.

Patrick was the club's first coach. He set a standard for all of those who followed him. The Rangers won the Stanley Cup in his second season behind the bench and again five years later. Patrick understood the sport of hockey as well as anyone in the world. If there was a small advantage to be had during a game, he would find it.

Patrick was known as an *innovator*. For example, he encouraged his three top scorers—Boucher, Bill Cook, and Bun Cook—to practice their passing and shooting separately from the team. This helped them experiment with plays that made them the best line in the NHL. Prior to the 1939–40 season, Patrick decided to focus on running the Rangers' business. He named Boucher head coach. Boucher led the club to its third Stanley Cup that spring.

Mike Keenan embraces the Stanley Cup in 1994 as the
Rangers celebrate around him.

New York's fourth Stanley Cup came 54 years later, under Mike
Keenan. He coached the Rangers for only a year—but what a year
it was! He whipped his players into championship form and made
them believe they were unbeatable. The Rangers won 52 games in
1993–94 and captured the Stanley Cup in a thrilling seven-game
series. Keenan was nicknamed "Iron Mike" because he was so tough
on his players.

ONE GREAT DAY

Is there such a thing as a team of destiny? The Rangers and their fans believed they were destined to win the Stanley Cup in the spring of 1994. Of course, in order to do so, New York had to make it to the Stanley Cup Finals—and the New Jersey Devils had something to say about that. The Devils led after five games in the conference finals. The Rangers were one loss away from an early exit from the playoffs.

New York captain Mark Messier knew he had to do something to get the attention of his teammates. The night before Game 6 in New Jersey, he told reporters, "We know we have to win it. We can win it. And we are going to win it."

The problem was that the Devils read the newspapers, too. With New Jersey fans screaming at the top of their lungs, the team built a 2–0 lead in the third period. The pressure was now on Messier. The Rangers made the score 2–1 when he flicked a pass

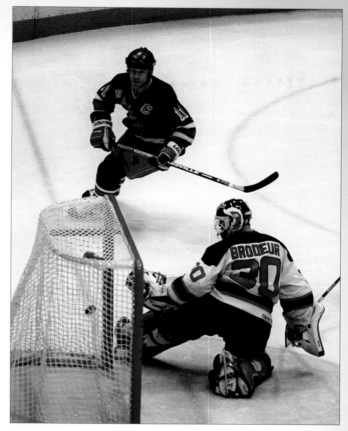

Martin Brodeur is helpless to stop Mark Messier's winning goal in Game 6.

to Alexei Kovalev, who shot the puck past goalie Martin Brodeur. The Rangers tied the score when Messier took a hard pass from Kovalev and tucked the puck under Brodeur's legs. New York took a 3–2 lead when Messier won a **faceoff** and then headed for the net. Brodeur stopped a shot by Kovalev, but Messier banged in the rebound. With time running out, the Devils pulled the goalie. Messier stopped a pass in front of his goal and calmly sent the puck skidding down the ice for his third goal of the game.

Two nights later, New York beat New Jersey in Game 7 in Madison Square Garden. The Rangers went on to win the Stanley Cup. Not only had Messier made good on his promise to beat the Devils, he delivered the first Stanley Cup to New York in more than 50 years.

LEGEND HAS IT

WHICH RANGER INVENTED THE CURVED HOCKEY STICK?

Andy Bathgate

LEGEND HAS IT that Andy Bathgate did. Bathgate actually began experimenting with this idea before he became a professional. He soaked the blade of his stick in hot water, bent it, and then let it dry overnight. Bathgate found that shooting with a curved stick made the puck do strange things in the air. Soon other NHL players were using curved sticks. Eventually, the league had to limit the curve of a stick for the safety of the goalies.

ABOVE: Andy Bathgate discovered that a curved stick blade made him an even better scorer.

DID FRANK BOUCHER COME UP WITH THE IDEA FOR THE RED LINE?

LEGEND HAS IT that he did. The red line is the center stripe on the ice, between the two blue lines. During the first 25 seasons in the NHL, the rules prevented passing over the blue line; a player had to carry the puck out of his own end. This slowed the game down tremendously. After coaching the Rangers to the Stanley Cup in 1940, Boucher joined the league's rules committee. In 1943, he convinced the NHL to add the red line. Teams could now pass from one zone to the next—as long as the pass did not also go across the red line.

WHICH RANGER WAS A BASEBALL HERO BEFORE HE PLAYED PRO HOCKEY?

LEGEND HAS IT that Chris Drury was. In 2008, Drury was named New York's captain. He was just the second American-born captain in team history. Nearly two decades earlier, Drury was a star in a different sport. In 1989, he led the baseball team from his hometown of Trumbull, Connecticut, to the Little League World Series. Trumbull won the championship thanks to Drury's pitching and hitting.

The secret dream of every NHL goalie is to score a goal. In Chuck Rayner's case, it was no secret at all. He was always on the lookout for an opportunity to put the puck in the net. In all of his years with the Rangers, Rayner never had a winning record.

Still, he was the most athletic and *agile* goalie in the league. In 1949–50, he went 28–30–11 and helped the Rangers reach the Stanley Cup Finals.

Rayner loved to join the Rangers' attack. He would skate to the other end of the ice when the referees called a **delayed penalty** on an opponent, hoping to surprise the goalie with a shot. Fans in Madison Square Garden loved watching their goalie transform into an offensive player.

Rayner once played in an exhibition match against the Maritime All-Stars in Canada. Since the game didn't count, he decided this was his big chance to realize his dream. He barreled down the ice

with the puck, shouldering opponents out of the way. Once he crossed the opposite blue line, Rayner cut to the net and backhanded a shot past the stunned goalie. He finally had his goal.

"I stopped a shot and the puck bounced straight out," he recalls. "I skated out to get clear, found myself alone and went the rest of the way. When I got about 15 feet from the other goal, I shot and scored."

More than two decades later, Rayner celebrated another thrilling moment in his career. In 1973, he became just the second goalie in hockey history with a losing record to be voted into the Hall of Fame.

LEFT: This trading card shows Chuck Rayner late in his career.
ABOVE: Rayner strays from his net to chase down the puck.

Rangers fans are unlike any others in the NHL. The crowd at games is made up of kids and old-timers, heads of large companies and everyday office workers, celebrities and celebrity-watchers. Some live a few blocks from Madison Square Garden, while others travel from other states to watch the team play. Once the puck drops, however, they cheer as one.

Rangers fans love hockey, and they understand the game. They applaud for players who work hard and do the little things to help the team win. If a player gives less than his all, he can expect to hear from the "coaches" in the stands. Barry Beck, who starred for the Rangers in the 1980s, said he hated to leave Madison Square Garden after a loss. "My doorman won't even talk to me!" he once claimed.

LEFT: The Rangers salute their fans after a game in Madison Square Garden.
RIGHT: New York fans bought this game program during the 1940s.

TIMELINE

The hockey season is played from October through June. That means each season takes place at the end of one year and the beginning of the next. In this timeline, the accomplishments of the Rangers are shown by season.

1939–40
The Rangers win their third Stanley Cup.

1966–67
Harry Howell wins the Norris Trophy.

1927–28
The Rangers win the Stanley Cup in their second season.

1958–59
Andy Bathgate becomes the team's first 40-goal scorer.

1976–77
Don Murdoch scores five goals in a game.

Bill Cook was a star for the 1928 champs.

This team photo shows the 1940 Stanley Cup.

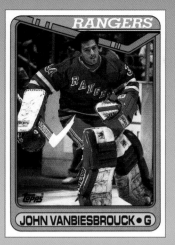

John
Vanbiesbrouck

Marian
Gaborik

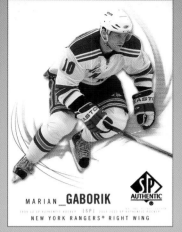

1985–86
John Vanbiesbrouck
wins the Vezina Trophy.

1993–94
The Rangers win
their first Stanley
Cup in 54 years.

2011–12
Marian Gaborik is
named MVP of the
All-Star Game.

1991–92
Mark Messier leads
the Rangers to their
first 50-win season.

2001–02
Theo Fleury scores his
1,000th career point.

2005–06
Jaromir Jagr sets a team
record with 54 goals.

Jaromir
Jagr

FUN FACTS

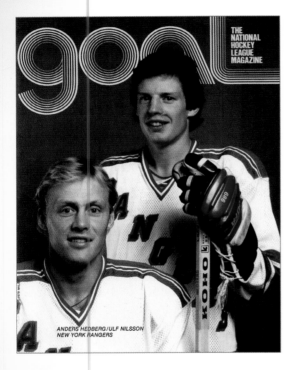

ANDERS HEDBERG/ULF NILSSON
NEW YORK RANGERS

SWEDISH CONNECTION

In 1978, the Rangers signed two stars from the **World Hockey Association (WHA)**, Anders Hedberg and Ulf Nilsson. Only two Swedes had played in the NHL before them.

UNDER FIRE

In a 1944 game against the Boston Bruins, New York goalie Ken McAuley set a record by stopping 86 shots. That made up for a game a month earlier, when the Detroit Red Wings scored 15 goals against him.

OK, WHO'S NEXT?

In 1966–67, Ed Giacomin led the NHL with nine **shutouts**. He had at least one against every team in the league.

FAMILY MATTERS

Where would the Rangers be without the Patrick family? Lester Patrick coached the team to two Stanley Cups. His sons, Lynn and Muzz, starred for the 1940 Stanley Cup winners. In the late 1980s, Lynn's son, Craig, signed many of the players that helped the Rangers win the Stanley Cup in 1994.

ART HISTORY

As of 2013, no Ranger had won the Art Ross Trophy as the league's top scorer. However, two Rangers won the scoring title before the award was given out—Bill Cook in 1926–27 and 1932–33, and Bryan Hextall in 1941–42.

DON'T GET SO DEFENSIVE

In 1993–94, New York's leading scorer was Sergei Zubov, with 89 points. It was the first time in NHL history that a defenseman was the top scorer on a first-place team.

LEFT: Anders Hedberg and Ulf Nilsson were front-page news in 1978.
ABOVE: Lester Patrick clowns around with his sons, Lynn and Muzz.

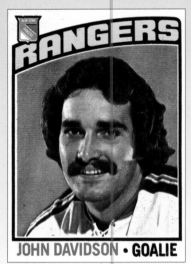

JOHN DAVIDSON • GOALIE

"If I get the chance, I like to shoot. But I always look to pass if there's an opportunity. I like to draw someone and set someone else up."

▶ **BRIAN LEETCH,** *on helping the team on offense*

"I had a lot of ability but was never as good as I should have been. In television, I was given a second chance."

▶ **JOHN DAVIDSON,** *on becoming an announcer for the Rangers after his playing days ended*

"The fans felt the only reason I made the Rangers was because my dad, Lester, was the big man."

▶ **LYNN PATRICK,** *on what made his 1942 goal-scoring championship extra sweet*

"Although we didn't get paid much, it was a lot of fun. We played with *intensity*."

▶ **BUN COOK,** *on pro hockey in the 1920s and 1930s*

"The Rangers are the most loved and hated team in hockey. Anywhere they go, city to city, the Rangers have a tremendous following of New Yorkers."

▶ **WAYNE GRETZKY,** *on the thrill of playing for the Rangers*

"We were part of something that hadn't been done in 54 years. It was an amazing time for us."

▶ **MARK MESSIER,** *on the 1994 Stanley Cup*

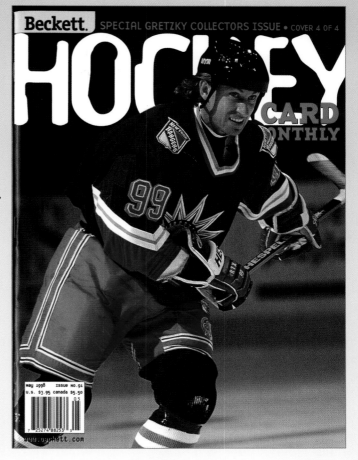

"I can't explain the feeling of winning the Stanley Cup. It's the ultimate."

▶ **CLINT SMITH,** *on the team's championship in 1940*

"The only job worse is javelin-catcher at a track and field meet!"

▶ **GUMP WORSLEY,** *on life as an NHL goalie*

LEFT: John Davidson
ABOVE: Wayne Gretzky

GREAT DEBATES

People who root for the Rangers love to compare their favorite moments, teams, and players. Some debates have been going on for years! How would you settle these classic hockey arguments?

MIKE RICHTER WAS THE TEAM'S ALL-TIME BEST GOALIE ...

... because he was in the net when the Rangers claimed their long-awaited 1994 championship. During his career, he won 301 games for the team in the regular season, and 41 more in the playoffs. Richter was small for a goalie, but his quick reflexes helped him cover the net like a giant. And he made some giant saves—including one on a penalty shot by Pavel Bure during the 1994 Stanley Cup Finals.

NO ONE WAS BETTER THAN EDDIE GIACOMIN ...

ED GIACOMIN

NEW YORK RANGERS

GOALIE

... because he lived up to his nickname year after year. "Steady Eddie" almost never made a bad play or mistake. When the Rangers needed an acrobatic save, he was ready. He was also considered one of the toughest and most courageous players in the NHL. Giacomin (LEFT) won 266 games for the Rangers, including 49 shutouts, and played in the All-Star Game five years in a row starting in 1967.

STEPHANE MATTEAU SCORED THE GREATEST OVERTIME GOAL IN TEAM HISTORY ...

... because it put the Rangers on a path to win the 1994 Stanley Cup. Matteau's wrap-around goal against the New Jersey Devils in Game 7 of the conference finals came in the second overtime period of a thrilling game. The celebration (RIGHT) was so exciting that announcer Howie Rose kept repeating, "Matteau! Matteau! Matteau!"

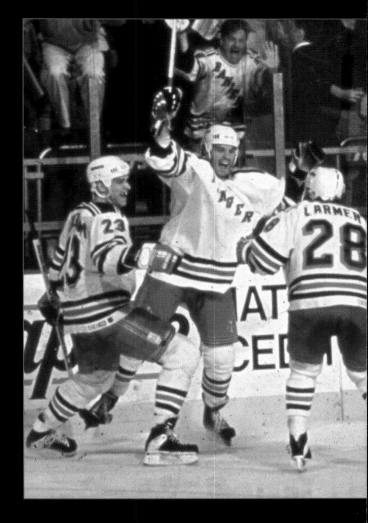

CHECK THE RECORD BOOKS. BRYAN HEXTALL DESERVES THAT HONOR ...

... because his overtime goal against the Toronto Maple Leafs in 1940 won the Stanley Cup. Hextall scored a little more than two minutes into the extra period to win the game 3–2 and deliver a championship to New York. Seriously—how do you beat that?

T he great Rangers teams and players have left their marks on the record books. These are the "best of the best" …

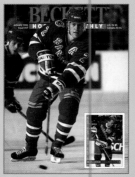

Steve Vickers

RANGERS AWARD WINNERS

HART MEMORIAL TROPHY
MOST VALUABLE PLAYER

Buddy O'Connor	1947–48
Chuck Rayner	1949–50
Andy Bathgate	1958–59
Mark Messier	1991–92

VEZINA TROPHY
TOP GOALTENDER

Davey Kerr	1939–40
Ed Giacomin & Gilles Villameure	1970–71
John Vanbiesbrouck	1985–86
Henrik Lundqvist	2011–12

JAMES NORRIS MEMORIAL TROPHY
TOP DEFENSEMAN

Doug Harvey	1961–62
Harry Howell	1966–67
Brian Leetch	1991–92
Brian Leetch	1996–97

ALL-STAR GAME MVP

Don Maloney	1983–84
Mike Gartner	1992–93
Mike Richter	1993–94
Wayne Gretzky	1998–99
Marian Gaborik	2011–12

CALDER TROPHY
TOP FIRST-YEAR PLAYER

Kilby MacDonald	1939–40
Grant Warwick	1941–42
Edgar Laprade	1945–46
Pentti Lund	1948–49
Gump Worsley	1952–53
Camille Henry	1953–54
Steve Vickers	1972–73
Brian Leetch	1988–89

CONN SMYTHE TROPHY
MVP DURING PLAYOFFS

Brian Leetch	1993–94

Brian Leetch

RANGERS ACHIEVEMENTS

ACHIEVEMENT	YEAR
Stanley Cup Champions	1927–28
Stanley Cup Finalists	1928–29
Stanley Cup Finalists	1931–32
Stanley Cup Champions	1932–33
Stanley Cup Finalists	1936–37
Stanley Cup Champions	1939–40
Stanley Cup Finalists	1949–50
Stanley Cup Finalists	1971–72
Stanley Cup Finalists	1978–79
Stanley Cup Champions	1993–94

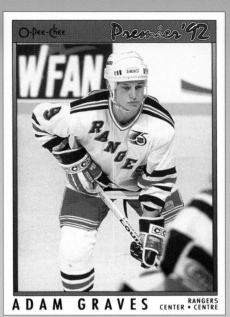

ADAM GRAVES   RANGERS CENTER • CENTRE

ABOVE: Adam Graves scored 52 goals for the 1994 champs.
LEFT: Davey Kerr was the goalie for the 1940 champs.
BELOW: Jean Ratelle was the team's top scorer in 1971–72.

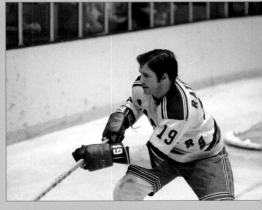

PINPOINTS

The history of a hockey team is made up of many smaller stories. These stories take place all over the map—not just in the city a team calls "home." Match the pushpins on these maps to the **TEAM FACTS**, and you will begin to see the story of the Rangers unfold!

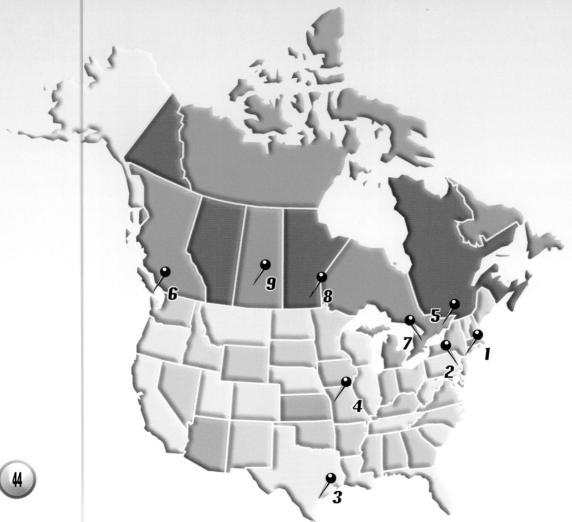

TEAM FACTS

1 New York, New York—*The Rangers have played here since 1926.*

2 Abington, Pennsylvania—*Mike Richter was born here.*

3 Corpus Christi, Texas—*Brian Leetch was born here.*

4 Kansas City, Missouri—*Tex Rickard was born here.*

5 Ottawa, Ontario—*John Davidson was born here.*

6 Victoria, British Columbia—*Lynn Patrick was born here.*

7 Brampton, Ontario—*Rick Nash was born here.*

8 Winnipeg, Manitoba—*Andy Bathgate was born here.*

9 Sutherland, Saskatchewan—*Chuck Rayner was born here.*

10 Åre, Sweden—*Henrik Lundqvist was born here.*

11 Moscow, Russia—*Sergei Zubov was born here.*

12 Kladno, Czech Republic—*Jaromir Jagr was born here.*

Lynn Patrick

GLOSSARY

AGILE—Quick and graceful.

ALL-STAR GAME—The annual game that features the best players from the NHL.

AMATEUR—Someone who plays a sport without being paid.

ASSISTS—Passes that lead to a goal.

CONFERENCE—A large group of teams. There are two conferences in the NHL, and each season each conference sends a team to the Stanley Cup Finals.

DECADES—Periods of 10 years; also specific periods, such as the 1950s.

DELAYED PENALTY—A penalty that does not take effect until the penalized team gains control of the puck.

DIVISION—A small group of teams in a conference. Each NHL conference has three divisions.

DYNASTY—A family, group, or team that maintains power over time.

ERA—A period of time in history.

FACEOFF—A battle for the puck that occurs after play stops. Two players "face off" against each other as the referee drops the puck between them.

GENERATION—A group of people born and living at approximately the same time.

HALL OF FAME—The museum in Toronto, Canada, where hockey's best players are honored. A player voted into the Hall of Fame is sometimes called a "Hall of Famer."

HAT TRICK—Three goals in a game.

INNOVATOR—Someone who is able to come up with new ideas.

INTENSITY—The strength and energy of a thought or action.

LINE—The trio made up by a left wing, center, and right wing.

LOGOS—Symbols or designs that represent a company or team.

MINOR LEAGUES—All the professional leagues that operate below the NHL.

MOST VALUABLE PLAYER (MVP)—The award given each year to the league's best player; also given to the best player in the playoffs and All-Star Game.

NATIONAL HOCKEY LEAGUE (NHL)—The professional league that has been operating since 1917.

OVERTIME—An extra period played when a game is tied after three periods. In the NHL playoffs, teams continue to play overtime periods until a goal is scored.

PLAYOFFS—The games played after the season to determine the league champion.

POSTSEASON—Another term for playoffs.

POTENTIAL—The possibility of achieving greater success.

PROFESSIONAL—A player or team that plays a sport for money.

ROSTER—The list of a team's active players.

SHUTOUTS—Games in which a team doesn't score a goal.

STANDINGS—A daily list of teams, starting with the team with the best record and ending with the team with the worst record.

STANLEY CUP—The trophy presented to the NHL champion. The first Stanley Cup was awarded in 1893.

STANLEY CUP FINALS—The final playoff series that determines the winner of the Stanley Cup.

TRADITION—A belief or custom that is handed down from generation to generation.

WESTERN CANADA HOCKEY LEAGUE (WCHL)—A league that operated in the western part of Canada during the 1920s.

WORLD HOCKEY ASSOCIATION (WHA)—The professional league that operated from 1972 to 1979.

LINE CHANGE

TEAM SPIRIT introduces a great way to stay up to date with your team! Visit our **LINE CHANGE** link and get connected to the latest and greatest updates. **LINE CHANGE** serves as a young reader's ticket to an exclusive web page—with more stories, fun facts, team records, and photos of the Rangers. Content is updated during and after each season. The **LINE CHANGE** feature also enables readers to send comments and letters to the author! Log onto:

www.norwoodhousepress.com/library.aspx

and click on the tab: **TEAM SPIRIT** to access **LINE CHANGE**.

Read all the books in the series to learn more about professional sports. For a complete listing of the baseball, basketball, football, and hockey teams in the **TEAM SPIRIT** series, visit our website at:

www.norwoodhousepress.com/library.aspx

ON THE ROAD

NEW YORK RANGERS
2 Pennsylvania Plaza
New York, New York 10121
(212) 465-6000
http://rangers.nhl.com

HOCKEY HALL OF FAME
Brookfield Place
30 Yonge Street
Toronto, Ontario, Canada M5E 1X8
(416) 360-7765
http://www.hhof.com

ON THE BOOKSHELF

To learn more about the sport of hockey, look for these books at your library or bookstore:

- Cameron, Steve. *Hockey Hall of Fame Treasures.* Richmond Hill, Ontario, Canada: Firefly Books, 2011.

- MacDonald, James. *Hockey Skills: How to Play Like a Pro.* Berkeley Heights, New Jersey: Enslow Elementary, 2009.

- Keltie, Thomas. *Inside Hockey! The legends, facts, and feats that made the game.* Toronto, Ontario, Canada: Maple Tree Press, 2008.

INDEX

PAGE NUMBERS IN **BOLD** REFER TO ILLUSTRATIONS.

THE TEAM

MARK STEWART has written over 200 books for kids—and more than a dozen books on hockey, including a history of the Stanley Cup and an authorized biography of goalie Martin Brodeur. He grew up in New York City during the 1960s rooting for the Rangers, but has gotten to know a couple of New Jersey Devils, so he roots for a shootout when these teams play each other. Mark comes from a family of writers. His grandfather was Sunday Editor of *The New York Times*, and his mother was Articles Editor of *Ladies' Home Journal* and *McCall's*. Mark has profiled hundreds of athletes over the past 25 years. He has also written several books about his native New York and New Jersey, his home today. Mark is a graduate of Duke University, with a degree in history. He lives and works in a home overlooking Sandy Hook, New Jersey. You can contact Mark through the Norwood House Press website.

DENIS GIBBONS is a writer and editor with *The Hockey News* and a former newsletter editor of the Toronto-based Society for International Hockey Research (SIHR). He was a contributing writer to the publication *Kings of the Ice: A History of World Hockey* and has worked as chief hockey researcher at five Winter Olympics for the ABC, CBS, and NBC television networks. Denis also has worked as a researcher for the FOX Sports Network during the Stanley Cup playoffs. He resides in Burlington, Ontario, Canada with his wife Chris.